BATHROOMS

BETA-PLUS

BATHROOMS
originally published in Dutch and French
BADKAMERS/SALLES DE BAINS

PUBLISHER
BETA-PLUS sa
Termuninck 3
7850 Enghien
Belgium
Tel : +32 (0)2 395 90 20
Fax : +32 (0)2 395 90 21
Website: www.betaplus.com
E-mail: betaplus@skynet.be

PHOTOGRAPHY
Jo Pauwels a.o. (photography credits p. 200)

LAYOUT
POLYDEM sprl
Nathalie Binart

TRANSLATION
Alexia Aughuet (Dutch to French)
Yvonne Lim and Serena Narain (French to English)

August 2005
ISBN: 907-721-340-6

NEXT
This bathroom was
designed by
Odile Dejaegere.
The floor in secular oak
is from Van Huele.

LEFT
Bathroom in an 18th century farm by artist Daan Van Doorn.

CONTENTS

PREFACE

During the past few years, bathrooms have begun to gain more importance in our interiors.

From a purely functional space, it has now been transformed into a place of refuge, a source of physical and mental well-being, and a haven of peace in our stressful existence.

An extremely relaxing and refreshing space, each bathroom is expressed in current classical style or contemporary minimalism. Interior architects and designers have, more than ever, proposed concepts that respond to individual needs, as well as to particular requirements of their clients. Harmony of colour tones, materials and styles play an essential role in the design of bathrooms.

This inspiring book serves to guide professional interior specialists as well as laymen in their choice of techniques, materials and fittings, for example, bath tubs, shower cubicles and accessories, natural stones, tiles, vanity counters, mirrors, lightings, etc.

Hundreds of recent photos illustrate the current trends in this particular domain.

CHAPTER I

INSPIRING CREATIONS BY INTERIOR ARCHITECTS

FUNCTIONALITY AND HARMONY
IN AN ELEGANT DESIGN

Impassioned and enthralling at the same time, Isabelle Bijvoet is a young interior architect from the region of Antwerp. She has transformed a small children room and a non-utilised space underneath the roof into an inspiring bathroom. Functionality, space, lighting, and intimacy are the strong concepts for this bathroom, thus creating a peaceful and meditative atmosphere.

Each detail in this bathroom witnesses the passion of Isabelle Bijvoet, where functionality and harmony are combined into an elegant design.

LEFT AND ABOVE

The Turkish hammam is one of the principle sources of inspiration in this work by Isabelle Bijvoet.

The colour of the floor resembles a carpet of pebbles from Chinese rivers that is cemented with white sand. The existing ceiling brought forth an arched ceiling installed by Gypel. The natural Moroccan tadellakt sand finish is realised by ART sprl.

The sink is Starck's signature and tap is from Vola. "Nobi" lighting is from Fontana Arte.
Accessories in oak are from Pomd'or (Novia).

LEFT AND ABOVE

From the bathtub (Starck), we have a beautiful view of the terrace and garden. In the day, the internal louver shutters bestow another dimension to the bathroom. In the evening, the lit-up niches accentuate the intimacy of the space. The custom-made oak cabinet with drawers offers practical shelving and arrangement space.

The long mirror has a fixed element and two pivoting ones.

The vanity counter is constructed on site and finished with waterproof Tadelakt.

FUNCTIONAL AND LIVABLE:
FIVE INSPIRING BATHROOMS

This article begins with the discovery of five recent completed works by interior design firm
Cy Peys / Partners.

LEFT AND ABOVE

This reserved but extremely functional bathroom was installed in an abode circa 1920. The two standing blocks
with embedded basin, custom-made in solid tropical essence wood, are placed against a free-standing, non-full
height partition that demarcates the bath from the shower area. Heating elements are integrated into the
black-colour floor.

Basins are from Corian and taps are designed by Arne Jacobsen.

The bathroom opens out to a terrace with a park view.

Left and Above

Bathtub in royal dimensions and shower are made-to-measure in black Corian, using same essence of wood as the basin vanity counter. Upon client's request, the shower head is embedded in the ceiling. A heating system has been integrated at the circumference of the bathtub.

The recess wall painted in glossy noir is equipped with a discreet lighting. The artworks are conceived by Cy Peys / Partners.

The children's bathroom is equipped with custom-made toilet furniture with a basin in bluestone. The mirror hides an indirect lighting. The shower cubicle, covered with white square tiles, is elevated and equipped with two shower points, one with fine jets and the other with massage jets for every child.

LEFT

Two abodes have been reunited to form a luxurious ensemble where all the family members can benefit from the facilities, which include the bathrooms. The independent bathtub in the parent's bathroom is wrapped in natural Italian stone, just like the one for the basin. The painted timber strips depict a Long Island atmosphere. All the furniture in the toilet is strictly without exposed handles and the floor is in oak wood. The window, which occupies the whole width of the niche, is occulted by the timber blinds that match the floor material.

NEXT

Upon the clients' request, no plinth is placed around the bathtub so as to accentuate its solidness.

LEFT AND ABOVE

The robust profile demarcates the shower cubicle, which is finished with white tiles and natural Italian stone.

A niche was envisaged on the wall for bath accessories.

NEXT
The hammam floor is in
natural French stone.
Directional lighting is
integrated in the ceiling.
Basins are embedded in
the surface in natural
stone. Mirror and toilet
furniture in timber
without apparent
handles. All bathroom
accessories are from
Waterl'Eau
Emery & Cie.

LEFT AND ABOVE

The works undertaken in this abode has permitted reduction of an over-sized entrance hall, which has allowed for the creation of an extremely functional hamman bathroom.

This space is accessible from the dressing room where the windows are. The bathtub measures from one wall to another. The teak floor is varnished. The existing window is provided with blinds. The uniform tones of colours confer a certain harmony to the whole.

The original flooring has been conserved in the children's bathroom. Here, shower and bath areas are combined as one.

Two rooms are joined together to form a large shower room with a dressing area. The separation is classical, however, it is modernised by Cy Peys / Partners thanks to a huge window placed in the wall.

LEFT

Despite the limited budget allocated for the transformation of this villa, the project on bathrooms nevertheless shows interesting architectural elements.

The bathroom on the second storey is conceived like a large shower space, isolated by a glass wall. Both the floor and walls are covered in black tiles.

SOBER TONES IN BATHROOMS OF TWO RESIDENCES AT THE COAST

With the passing years, interior architect Bert Desmet has acquired an excellent reputation as creator of contemporary and timeless interiors.

This article shows the bathrooms from two of his works: one in an exclusive apartment at Knokke-le-Zoute (p. 32-37) and the other in a villa in Oostduinkerke (p. 38-41).

P. 32-35

In these two bathrooms in an apartment situated in Knokke-le-Zoute, Bert Desmet has opted for a palette of sober tones and durable materials: Dominique Desimpel's beach pebbles for the floor and wall above the basins, oak for the shutters and bathtub coverings, and solid Anthalia marble for the basin. Tap fittings are from Dornbracht.

LEFT AND ABOVE

A Securit glass wall separates the spacious shower cubicle, which is covered entirely in pebbles.

LEFT AND ABOVE

An authentic fisherman house has been transformed into a modern holiday residence. The bathroom offers a warm and serene atmosphere due to the use of acid-treated Carrara marble, oak timber flooring and pinewood panelling for the floor and ceiling. Tap fittings are from Dornbracht.

Slates in the children's bathroom are from Dominique Desimpel. The basin is in solid limestone from Corton.

The hammam is covered with ceramic mosaic from Paray.

A SCANDINAVIAN AMBIENCE

The team of architects from AIDarchitecten realises various projects in Belgium and other countries. Their specific approach is characterised by various constants: respect for the environment, faith in architecture, durability and poetry, which are some of the indispensable ingredients. The true motivation is the person himself and the quality of life: styles and trends are secondary.

Contemporary bathrooms clearly exceed the utilitarian functionality: these are spaces delegated for the body and spirit, they are the spaces reserved for well-being.

This approach is well-illustrated in these two projects by interior designer Kristl Bakermans and architect Gerd Van Zundert.

LEFT AND ABOVE

Utilisation of natural materials (Azul Casais natural stone and oak wood) creates a Scandinavian atmosphere in this bathroom located in a country house in the suburbs of Antwerp.

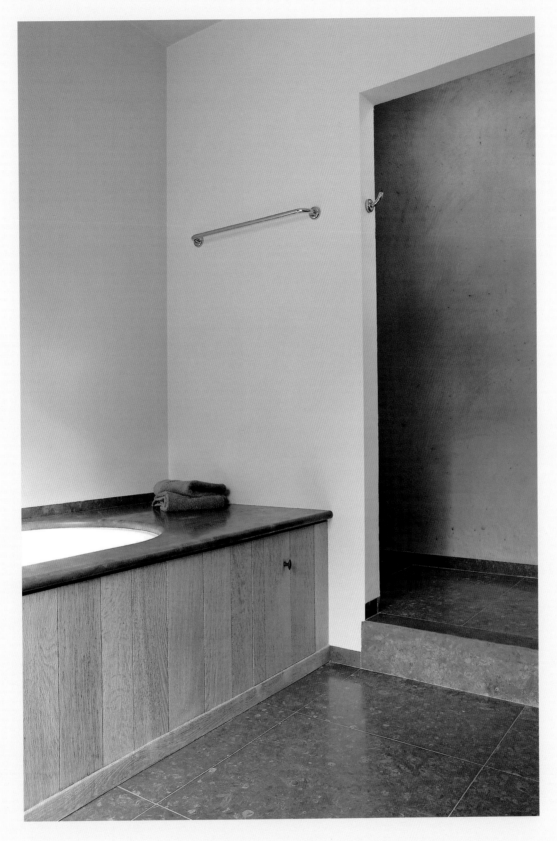

AIDarchitecten wants to express the essence of bath in a simple manner: 'undesigning the bath'.

LEFT AND ABOVE

Walls of the shower cubicle are finished with vapour-proof Moroccan plaster.

LEFT AND ABOVE

The unique situation of this boat-like abode being next to a lake inspires the Scandinavian ambience of this
bathroom.

LEFT AND THIS PAGE

Basin and bathtub are covered with Pietra Piasentina
natural stone, complemented by painted hard pine.
The shower area is finished with vapour-proof
Moroccan plaster.

EACH BATHROOM TELLS A STORY

It has been a number of years since Anne De Visscher and her husband, Eric Meert created an enterprise known as "Il était une fois.." in Brussels. With each passing year, the enterprise has further developed its specialisation of kitchens and craft-design bathrooms.

All bathrooms done by the enterprise witness a timeless radiation and are realised according to the strictest quality norms. Totally tailored-made, the bathrooms are equally adapted to the living routines of the client, meeting his or her desires at the start of each new concept. The furniture is painted only after installation, which allows greater flexibility in the choice of colours, as is clearly testified in the works illustrated here.

<small>NEXT
"The Sleeping Lake". The tones of white range towards the beige panelling and cement squares. The murals remind us of the fogs from the Northern sea.</small>

<small>LEFT AND ABOVE</small>
In this master house of the start of the previous century, "Il était une fois…" has introduced a contemporary note in a timeless classical whole. It is a space truly dedicated to relaxation. An ancient bathtub (Nirvana) sits on a custom-made plinth made of mahogany wood, in the middle of an oval floor surface in bluestone that creates an ambience that resembles bathing in Parma fog.

P.56-57

In this toilet, the Napoleonean-inspired furniture from "L'Ocean" is combined with a "L'Enfant Gâté" modern shower cubicle, and by its chrome tubes and clear glass plays an alternation to the polished and softened blue stone.

Walls and furniture are painted in the range of mauve and Parma. Same tones and pointed tiles are found in the window decorations.

P.58-59

"Cottage"- harmony of different wood essences (oak, afrormosia) and painted panelling with patinated pieces of furniture in beige give the roofs a warm and very intimate outlook.

Since always, "Il était une fois.." tells stories. Each bathroom is a tale itself: for this reason, "Il était une fois.." has given a name to each project. This article illustrates a few remarkable bathroom projects by the Brussels enterprise.

P.60-63
A "Zen" model.

An original creation of the owner and his architect. The musical setting of colours, Tadelakt and marmorino coatings, orchestrated by "Il 'etait une fois..".

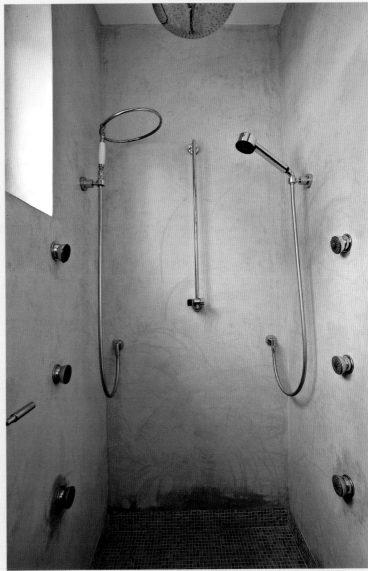

CHAPTER II

TIMELESS BATHROOMS

SECULAR PATINS IN A RESTORED SQUARE FARM

Virginie & Odile Dejaegere have designed the interior of a restored square farm in Wallonia.

By choosing ancient floors, a solid bathtub, and lime-washed walls, etc, they have conferred a secular patina to this unique farm.

LEFT

This bathroom, with its solid bathtub in marble, has become a place to live in. The secular floor is from Van Huele.

LEFT AND THIS PAGE
The basin and shower are equipped with tap fittings from Volevatch. The solid basin, the vanity counter and the shower floor are realised in bluestone.

EXUBERANT AND RICH IN COLOUR : BATHROOMS OF TWO COUNTRY HOUSES IN THE SOUTH OF FRANCE

Dutch interior designer Bert Quadvlieg is internationally appreciated for his exuberant interiors where durable materials, variegated colours and furniture inspired from antiques form a harmonious whole.

In this article, Quadvlieg allows us to discover bathrooms under his care in two marvellous country houses: the first in Théoule-sur-Mer and the second at Grasse.

NEXT
Above the bathtub, a Buxy blue natural stone slab forms part of the wall finish, from which a shell from Celebes is supported. The vanity counter of the basin and the backdrop wall are also in Buxy stone. Taps are from Lefroy Brooks. Between the cupboards, the wall is finished in 10 x 10 terracotta tiles. All timber works are in Java Teak; the walls feature several lime-washed layers. The terracotta floor is combined with large slabs of bluestone.

LEFT AND ABOVE
Behind the bathtub, the wall is covered in enamelled octagon tiles of Italian blue and yellow. A Heritage bathtub with tap fittings from Lefroy Brooks. The floor is finished in traditional terracotta.

The floor and a portion of the wall are covered with stones from Bali. Handwash basin is in timber and painted in white.
A mirror with a frame formed in wooden drifts is mounted above it.

LEFT
This bathroom is conceived for a country house at Grasse. The Carrara tiles alternate with Verde Vecchio marble.
The timber wall has received several layers of colours with old pigments. Bathtub is from Heritage and tap fittings
are from Lefroy Brooks. Antique mirror in a timber frame.

The wall above the Indonesian cabinet and vanity counter where the basin sits is covered with Buxy stone and marble tiles from Bali. Basin from Detremmerie. Copper tap fittings from Barthel.

NEXT
This Provence-style bathroom combines Amarello marble and shell limestone. The timber works are painted with a relief in two layers of patina. Tap fittings are from Lefroy Brooks.

LEFT
The corner handwash basin vanity with cabinet door panels in natural oak has a countertop in bluestone. Tap fittings from Barthel. Wall tiles are from Salernes in France. The floor, composed of terracotta tiles, features eight different tones.

EXCLUSIVE RAYS

The society Costermans Villaprojecten has
conceived and realised the bathrooms of a
spacious house situated in the green belt
surrounding Antwerp.

The contractor of the Schilde houses does
not hesitate in generously choosing durable
materials: exclusive French marbles,
original tap fittings, etc.

LEFT AND ABOVE

In this parent's bathroom, the bathtub is located in the centre with the shower cubicle on the left and toilet on the
right, behind the wall. Original French natural stone is everywhere: sand-coloured floor in marble from Hauteville
(softened finish) and a bathtub in polished black marble from Saint-Laurent.

The wall cabinet with an ebony frame is embedded in the wall. Tap fittings and lighting are from Dornbracht ("Madison Flair" series).

The children's bathroom combines a floor in natural stone from Hauteville and a handwash basin in antique red marble. Walls of the shower area are covered in marble mosaic and floor in antique red marble. Tap fittings are from Damixa ("Tradition" series). Door panels of the cabinet and framing of the mirror cabinet are in water-resistant MDF.

SERENITY AND INTIMACY

Architect Stephane Boens has conceived a marvellous country house inspired by an English-style in the green belt zones next to Antwerp.

In this unique decor, the bathrooms created provide an image of habitation that breathes space, serenity and intimacy.

Natural stone and tiles in this bathroom are delivered by Dominique Desimpel.

BEAUTY AND REFINEMENT
IN TWO BATHROOMS

Renowned interior specialist, Walda Pairon has created two designs of bathrooms that totally correspond to his universe: a harmonious fusion of old and new, with a passion for durable materials, warm colours and exclusive variety of natural stone and timber.

Lamps and serviette holders are conceived by Walda Pairon. A mirror of the 18th century is designed in an ebony frame.

Left

A bathtub made out of cast-iron. Taps are from Pendragon. Blinds are in cotton and an antique pouffe-table completes the décor.

Wall and floor finish in the shower cubicle is in bluestone from Belgium.

LEFT

The floor in beech wood has been painted. To the left, a console in pinewood with an academic hand-shaped plaster sculpture.

For this bathroom, Walda Pairon has utilised a very exclusive marble that originated from an exhausted quarry in Brecchia: for the floor, handwash basin covering and around the bathtub. All these are combined with Carrara white on the walls. Faithful to the secular Italian process, the painter has applied Coristil paints with a technique that produces very beautiful walls that are entirely washable.

DISCREET LUXURY AND INTIMATE CHARM

Passionate about decorating, the three brothers of Flamant and their team create objects and furniture that seem to have always been in existence.

With a very precise sense of the authenticity, Flamant Home Interiors has invented a simple yet brilliant concept: the re-edition of old furniture and objects, re-adapted to suit today's needs. A mixture of styles that come from England, to the exoticism of the colonies, while passing by the Scandinavian style or style of the Provence.

The lines remain, however, very current. The universe of Flamant is one of discreet luxury and intimate charm. It is a perfect combination of personal comfort and renewal.

A wide range of bath products.   A Bocage bathtub.

LEFT
Flamant Bathrooms: a unique mix of old and new.

Serviette and bath towels from the "Home" collection. Baskets and boxes are from the "Havanah" series.

THIS PAGE
Two cabinets with integrated basins are from Calife: in old oak and painted white.

A Florence glass cabinet and the other in dark grey from Garonne.

LEFT
A Julia mirror surmounts a Dunbar bathroom furniture.

A bathrobe from Home insigne blue.

Bathroom furniture painted in Calife white.

A bath brush.   Bath gel from Histoire de Bain 1 L.

At times an interior designer, sometimes a furniture creator and other times a decorator, Flamant Home Interiors always has the adequate response, adapted to suit the client's requirements. One leg anchored in the past while the other in modernity; they are perfectly in harmony with current comfort.

All Flamant shops devote a lot of attention to the bathroom. There, visitors find all bath products: toilet furniture in natural timber either patinated or covered in natural stone, bathrooms furniture, mirrors, soap holders, bathroom linen and a complete range of bath products and other products for the well-being.

CHAPTER III

CONTEMPORARY BATHROOMS

A CURRENT BATHROOM IN A RESIDENCE FROM THE 16TH CENTURY

In the historic heart of Antwerp, two master houses have been transformed into an elegant urban hotel known as l'Hotel Julien.

The owner, Mouche Van Hool, called upon AIDarchitecten (Kristl Bakermans and Gerd Van Zundert).

The layout of the rooms have been reviewed to create eleven spacious hotel rooms with superb bathrooms. In the restoration process, important historic elements were conserved and honoured. The interior installation privileges sober lines and colours, which accentuate existing architecture and historical details.

LEFT

The terracotta tiles were recovered from a 7th century building. Bathroom and handwash basin cabinet are in oak and covered with natural stone from Massangis.

LEFT AND THIS PAGE
The nobility of Carrara
harmonises with the
robustness of solid oak
and restored historical
materials.

BATHROOMS IN TWO RESTORED RESIDENCES

This article presents two recent bathrooms conceived by young Brussels architect Olivier Dwek.

In a loft of an industrial building situated in Brussels, Dwek has created, with the collaboration of Mathieu Dewitte and Julie Ruquois, a bathroom that illustrates his taste in raw materials: the walls are finished in waterproof cement and the floor in concrete.

A sliding door with invisible handles hides away the toilet. On the left is the access to the shower.

LEFT
Two basins from Starck sit on a 'floating' vanity counter made of dark tinted timber. "Tara" tap fittings are from Dornbracht. "Nomade Minimal" application is from Modular.

B&H immobilien has requested Olivier Dwek and Gregory Eyndels to restore a Brussels abode of 1903 (P. 110-111). The original bricks have been sanded and furnished with an anti-dust varnish. The authentic floor has received a darker tint.

LEFT
Placed in the centre is a Bathline Concept Colombe bathtub in sandstone with tap fittings from Ritmonio. Above the basin vanity counter (with integrated heat-radiating grills and basins from Kusabi Basin) is a photo of Thomas Defays from Young Gallery.

OPEN AND SERENE

Interior designer Nathalie Van Reeth has transformed several exquisite rooms in three large spaces to accommodate the parent's bathroom, children's bathroom and the guest bathroom.

A monastic and sober atmosphere brings upon an image that bears Nathalie Van Reeth's signature: warm materials, stainless steel in matte finish, sandstone tiles and cement walls create an almost ascetic quietude.

LEFT AND ABOVE

Solid sandstone basin sits on two custom-made porcelain bases and is equipped with two Boffi taps. The walls are in cement finish and big sandstone slabs. The mirror has a stainless steel frame.

Timber panelling and cement walls for the children's bathroom. A timber vanity counter holds the basins and serviettes. Small brackets in stainless steel. The floor is painted. The old bathtub was made-to-measure with its timber legs painted white. Tap fittings are from Boffi.

LEFT
The ceramic bathtub is embedded in a natural stone case. Taps are from Boffi. The original heaters were repainted in a cement tone. First Edition Eames chairs.

LEFT AND ABOVE

Nathalie Van Reeth has conceived the guest bathroom like a large open space. The floor, bathtub and the basin are finished with sandstone. Solid bathtub with stop water inspired by Oriental designs. Wall lamp from Kreon, Boffi taps and prison toilet bowl in stainless steel.

A PASSION FOR DESIGN
AND REFINEMENT TECHNIQUES

It has been 40 years since Obumex has combined refinement techniques and the passion for pure aesthetics. The company conceives and realises a durable space and quality for each daily routine. Obumex is as involved in new construction as it is in renovation projects, where it either executes or co-ordinates.

Obumex Design Store offers the client a large assortment of designer furniture with renowned brands at international levels, such as B&B Italia, Maxalto, Christian Liagre, Promemoria, Knoll, Tecno, Vitra and Fantoni.

This article presents two bathroom projects by Obumex.

LEFT AND ABOVE

In this bathroom, the floor in oak is combined with "Trois jaune" natural stone. Tap fittings are from Dornbracht ("Tara" series).

LEFT AND THIS PAGE
This bath and shower
space has received a
granite finish from
Wolfgang Zobel (Lupo).

KNOW-HOW
CRAFT-DESIGN

A REPUTATION CAST IN STONE

For many years, Philippe Van Den Weghe is appreciated by architects and renowned designers as the specialist when it comes to exclusive realisations in natural stone. We recognise him not only for his special flair for new trends, but also as an exceptional know-how and a true passion for the trade.

Founded in 1978, his enterprise has more than 20 collaborators today and is one of the first to propose sublime stones like Pietra Piasentina, Buxy, Corton and Lava Stone.

Without the least compromise, Van Den Weghe constantly searches for the best quality, be it for treatment to natural stone or for works installed on site: his collaborators are considered to be the best specialists in this domain.

This article allows the discovery of four recently completed bathrooms that illustrate the excellence of the Van Den Weghe enterprise.

P.124-133

This is the last work of famous interior designer Jean De Meulder, who passed away at the start of construction.

The site was taken over by Stavit Mor Interiors and architect Frank Van Laere.

In the principal bathroom, the large bathtub in Dolomite Grun, which acts both like a Jacuzzi and a double shower, attracts all the attention. Thanks to the home automation system, we can refill the bathtub at a desired temperature via telephone.

Left
The walls of this steam shower are covered with mosaic tiles. The solid benches with integrated ambience lighting are finished in Dolomit Grun.

P.130-131

In the same residence, the guest bathroom is finished in softened Crema Marfil Stone. The bathtub and the basin are entirely made of marble.

P.132-133
In the son's bathroom, we have
opted for grey Basaltina lava
stone, and the same material is
also used for the solid basin. The
shower cubicle walls are finished
in metal mosaic.

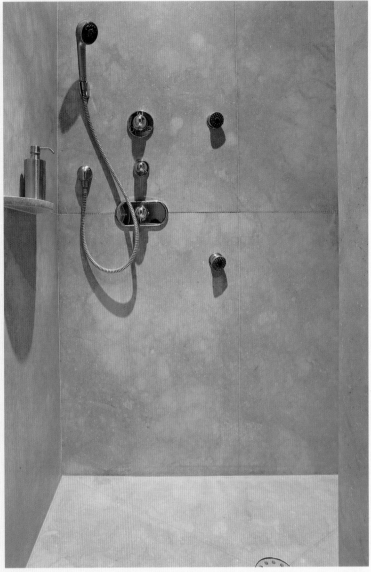

P.134-137

Brigitte Peten has conceived this bathroom as a livable space. Based on colours of the painting hung above the bathtub and of the yellowish tones of marble, the Brussels decorator has harmonised the colours and décor. Spanish Ambar marble, in a softened version, is provided and installed by Van Den Weghe.

P.138-139

The architect Brigitte Verstraete has combined a teak floor and pieces of White Quartz marble from Indonesia.

Van Den Weghe provides this material directly on the walls, which guarantees a perfect look.

P.140-141

Van Den Weghe created this superb bathroom in softened Lasa white marble, nearly without stains. The basins, walls and rounded steps are in solid marble. This is a very strong concept by Martine Cammaert (C&C Designburo).

MDC Meubles realised the joinery and Estrikor tended the celing with different lightings.

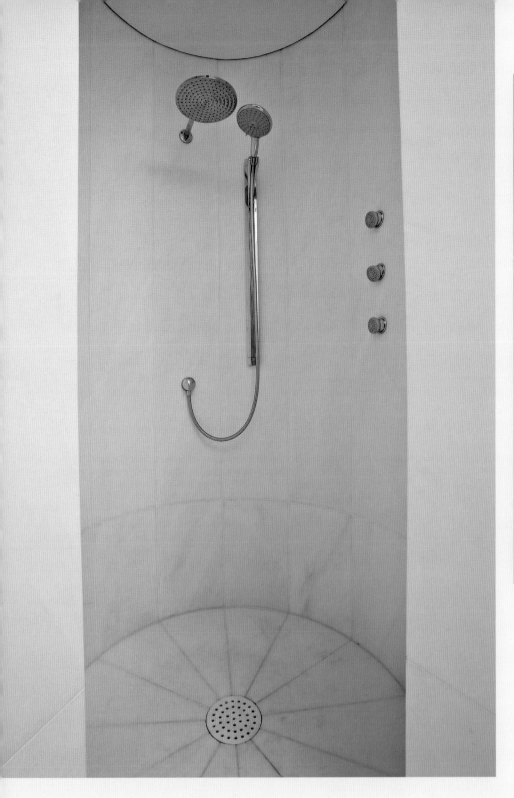

A PASSION
FOR CRAFT-DESIGN TILES

In 1985, Dominique Desimpel launched a trade of craft-design tiles.

In his shops at Knokke, he presents the most beautiful handmade tiles for wall and floor: handmade
enamelled terracotta and marble mosaic, authentic Moroccan slates, pebbles from the beach
and river, etc.

The important thing is not as much the origin but more
a characteristic timeless style.

Many exigent clients, renowned architects, interior
designers and decorators are refusing industrial style and
non-personal machine-made tiles, opting instead for a
preference towards tiles that provide poetry and
sensuality.

P.144-146
Slates, tiles, natural stone and pebbles utilised in the two projects by interior designer Philip Simoen were delivered
by Dominique Desimpel.

Architect Stéphane Boens shows a palette of almost monochrome natural stone in this work.

Design of bathroom and shower cubicle with river pebbles by interior designer Bert Desmet.

SOBER BEAUTY

It was in 1997 that Luc Lormans started De Menagerie, an enterprise that has in little time, created a passion in the production of high quality craft-design kitchens. His concept is distinguished by pure aesthetics and his choice of durable materials without concessions to trends.

For quite a while, Luc Lormans has also proposed concepts and realised bathrooms in a style we call "the livable minimalism": sober lines, monochrome palette, sensuous and warm materials, and an aestheticism that combines functionality with sober beauty.

The bathroom presented in this article is a recent work by De Menagerie that perfectly illustrates this approach.

P.148-151

A bathroom in a standard contemporary style created and realised by De Menagerie: a perfect symbiosis of quality materials (grey Catalan, tap fittings exclusive from Volevatch), brilliant functionality (layout of the bathroom and shower, clever storage areas, etc) and extremely sober and timeless design.

SECULAR EXPERIENCE
AND UNIQUE KNOW-HOW

The company Lerou is one of the oldest enterprises in Belgium. Their first works are dated as early as 1792! With the passing years, Lerou has built himself a very solid reputation: entrepreneurs, architects and interior decoration specialists appreciate unanimously the know-how, the genius technique and the respect for authenticity of the Brugean enterprise.

Lerou owns a wide range of bathroom accessories within a large variety of materials. Tap fittings that admirably complete this assortment are from Samuel-Heath. This English fabricator has, since 1820, produced taps for bathrooms, kitchens, cloakrooms and bidets, as well as a whole range of accessories for bathrooms and showers. As much as Lerou guarantees authenticity, quality in technique and impeccable finish of all its products, its collaboration with Samuel-Heath is a good testament: Lerou has been distributing a complete assortment from Samuel-Heath for over three decades.

Olive doorknob is forged on a rhombus plate and is typically painted in the same colour as the door.

LEFT AND THIS PAGE
A small handwash basin set with three elements from Samuel-Heath in antique gold.

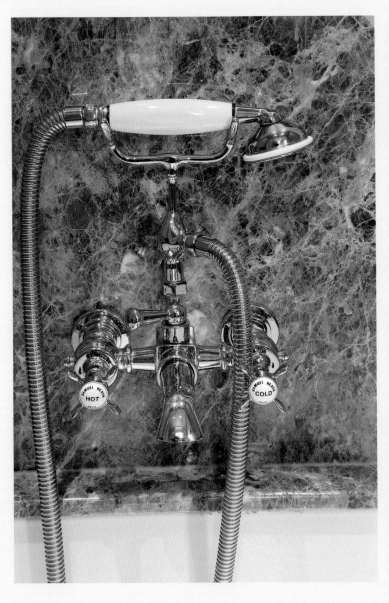

P.154-155
Bath/shower fittings in antique gold from Samuel-Heath form a wall montage.

The fabrication of taps and shower heads in solid brass guarantees a durable finish. Tap fittings are proposed in different finishes: polished chrome, polished nickel, silver, antique gold, gilded, polished brass, sylt, etc. These finishes are found in Lerou produces its very own range of accessories in solid brass, cast iron or porcelain. All finishes, colours or motifs are possible: from a simple cloth hanger to a basin, from serviette holders to lit mirrors or holders for cosmetic products and serviettes, etc. Many accessories can be custom-made.

Far from momentary trends, Lerou has for many years, provided high quality taps and accessories. It does not concentrate on the passing "retro" style, which after a while may no longer in production, but instead produces authentic products whose values do not cease to increase. As such the Brugean enterprise, together with Samuel-Heath, offers a guarantee and perfect after-sales service.

P.156-157
Like all the tap fittings from
Samuel-Heath, this small handwash
basin set in antique gold is available
in different styles. Here, the set is in
Victorian style but the taps are also
available in Georgian (handles in
porcelain), Art Deco, etc.

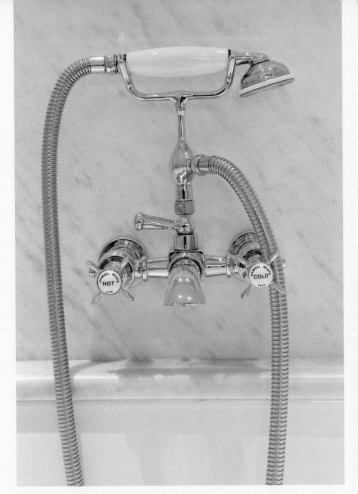

LEFT AND ABOVE

Bath/shower tap fittings in antique gold for wall assembly, with a hand shower also in antique gold.

An olive doorknob is forged on a rhombus plate with a rusty finish that matches the key.

Moreover, Lerou proposes other accessories for the bathroom: all furniture garnishes, ventilation grills, door fittings, rods, accessories in porcelain, etc.

Realised in the bathrooms of Chateau de Spycker Hotel in Bruges, this article shows numerous Samuel-Heath products. Lerou has provided the door fittings and other diverse accessories.different styles: Victorian, King George, Art Deco and Lillie Langtry, etc. and fit perfectly into a timeless bathroom.

All the versions imported by Lerou are equipped with the most recent technology in terms of ceramic treatment and conform to standard continental measurements. This indeed facilitates installation and maintenance. We can ask for British models as well as American models. The shower fittings are available in countless combinations. Lerou also proposes its very own assortment of accessories, which allows all sorts of implementations while still respecting the same style: fixed to the ceiling and combined with bathtub fittings, side jets, etc.

P.160-161
Different basin taps with cruciform handles in polished brass and with standard nozzle. They can fit into different environments: bathrooms, cloakrooms, etc.

THE MAGIC OF TADELAKT SECULAR TECHNIQUE

Jan Vanderbeken, founder of Odilon Creations, has been an enthusiastic defender of the Moroccan Tedelakt technique for many years. With his daughter Sigrid, he has followed the teachings of grand Maalem Mohammed, who in Atlas had entrusted them with his secrets.

In its primitive form, Tadelakt recognises many applications: Turkish bath, hammams, etc. Until today, the applications concern the walls, floors, bathroom equipments and baths, etc. for exterior as much as for interior, and for showers and basins, etc.

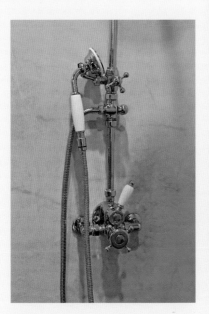

This open shower is realised in Tadelakt: a finish strictly in good quality and fine touch.
Realisation: Odilon Creations / Tadelakt Colours

LEFT
The walls are in Tadelakt finish with a light "Terre de Sienne" colour.

RIGHT
Thee portion above the basin is in Tadelakt grey: a colour that complements the basin in old bluestone. The paste, a mixture of lime and water is coloured with powder pigment. Thus the colours become more vibrant.
Realisation: Odilon Creations / Tadelakt Colours.

The very soft materials harden patiently in the hands. The smooth and silky walls give dimension to a warm atmosphere. Tadelakt offers many advantages: it is water and damp-proof, as well as heat-resistant.

The paste, a mixture of lime and water, is coloured with powder pigment. Thus the colours become more vibrant.

P.166-167

This minimalist bathroom was conceived by architect Piet De Mey. The floor is in polished concrete. The walls are in Tadelakt grey whereby the shades vary according to natural lighting.

The concrete basins are cast on site. Odilon Creations has covered all Tadelakt grey in the concrete aspect.

The shower area is also in Tadelakt. The cemented support is covered with a waterproof substance before the application of polished Tadelakt with black roller and soap. The three integrated halogen spotlights create a felted lighting.

P.168-169

This bathroom creation by Marie-Sophie Hubert (ETAU architecture firm) is a harmony of wood and turquoise Tadelakt

Contemporary elements (white porcelain basin, acrylic white bathtub and chrome tap fittings) contrast with the secular Tadelakt technique in this work by Odilon Creations / Tadelakt Colours. The Tadelakt technique not only creates an effect with a play on perspective, it also offers a protection against humidity.

In the shower, the Tedalakt technique was applied on a cement surface. The colour palette is developed with natural pigments of different colours.

This Geraldine Pauwels project is realised by Odilon
Creations / Tadelakt Colour. A layer of special cement
and another layer of waterproof protection are applied
in an Ytong construction. Walls and floors of the
shower area are finished in grey Tadelakt anthracite.
The basin cast on site has received a Tadelakt finish in
the same grey tone.

A PASSION FOR NATURAL STONE

For three generations, the Louis Culot enterprise from Londerzeel has enjoyed an excellent reputation in the natural stone sector. Thanks to Louis Culot who has led the enterprise since 1982, the company has become a PME with an employment of over 20 people.

In addition to Louis Culot's great specialty (natural stone in kitchens), his strength is also very much applied in bathrooms. Whether it is tiles, coverings of bathtubs, basins or showers, the Londerzeel enterprise offers a large choice of varieties in terms of models and finishes.

P.172-174

In this bathroom/shower, cement floor and walls were combined with Basaltina lava stone and made-to-measure by Louis Culot. Conception: W. Van Aggelpoel.

The floor, massive shower cubicle and the basins are made of Pietra Topaz Grisato, a limestone with sober tone.

P.176-177

In this bathroom, natural timber parquet was combined
with softened Carrara marble.

P.178-179

Subtle shades in perfect harmony with bathtub finish, shower and vanity counter in yellow French Massangis.
The tiles are in the same stone finish.

The fame of Louis Culot and his team lies on their professional approach, impeccable service,
competitive prices and quality of their works.

Handwash basin in black granite, "Black I", with mitre joints. Same method applies to the drawer.

LEFT AND ABOVE
This remarkable bathtub is cast on site and made-to-measure by Louis Culot in softened yellow Massangis.

Realisation: Architect B. Bladt.

QUALITY TAP FITTINGS
AND ACCESSORIES FOR BATHROOMS

Waterl'Eau is the original name of a bathroom shop opened in 1993 in Antwerp that proposes tap fittings, basins, bathtubs and exclusive bath accessories with a classic contemporary look.

The success of this shop has driven the founders to launch their very own bath gel/foam in 1996, thus the "Waters of the World" collection was born. In 2005, this range of products is introduced in numerous countries around the world.

LEFT AND ABOVE

In this bathroom, Dejaegere Interiors has chosen Volevatch tap fittings from the series "Lyre" (photo on the left and top right) and from the "Bistrot" collection (top left).

LEFT AND ABOVE

A work by architect Vincent Van Duysen with tap fittings from Volevatch, "Bistrot" series.

Another important activity by Waterl' Eau is the exclusive import and distribution of high quality French brand, Volevatch, which is produced in three timeless and current series ("Bistrot", "Carpe" and "Lyre") and is available in different finishes.

This article presents some recent works of bathroom projects with Volevatch tap fittings.

In this bathroom by decorator, Marijke Van Nunen, the choice of tap fittings is made on the "Bistrot" range.

"Carpe" tap fittings from
Volevatch by Bert Quadvlieg.

NATURAL STONE AND TILES
IN ALL DIMENSIONS

The firm Desloover Carrelages et Pierre Naturelle from Audenarde is a sure factor in the Belgian tile and natural stone sector for many years.

The enterprise proposes large assortments of elegant and high quality tiles for wall and floor. In addition, Desloover Carrelages et Pierre Naturelle also specialises in custom-made works in natural stone: handwash basin vanity tops, interfaces of shower wall, solid basins, coverings of bathtub, etc.

Desloover Carrelages et Pierre Naturelle is also a good address for the complete conception of bathrooms. Thanks to its creative and professional approach, the enterprise offers an appreciative importance. The workshop and experience personnel of Desloover Carrelages et Pierre Naturelle guarantee impeccable works. Maintenance and after-sales service are as important.

LEFT AND ABOVE

In these bathrooms, Desloover has delivered and installed Carrara white marble for the vanity counter and the wall finish in the shower cubicle.

P.190-191

When it comes to tiles, marble mosaic or natural stone, Desloover Carrelages et Pierre Naturelle satisfies all requirements.

The client is serviced from the tile or natural stone selection right up to the maintenance period. Experienced personnel, quality and service are the three main values in Desloover Carrelages et Pierre Naturelle.

BIBLIOGRAPHY

- Terence Conran, "Salles de bains: les plaisirs de l'eau". Hachette, 2004.
- Françoise Segall, "Salles de bains - chambres - salons - cuisines". Flammarion, 2003.
- Aldo Franchini, "Salles de bains". Actes Sud / Motta, 2004.
- Brad Mee, "Bathrooms: Design is in the Details". Chapelle, 2004.
- Françoise de Bonneville, "Le Livre du Bain". Flammarion, 2001.
- Fikret Yegul, "Baths and Bathing in Classical Antiquity". MIT Press, 1992-1996.
- Vinny Lee, "Bathrooms - Creative Planning for Beautiful Bathrooms". Ryland Peters & Small, 2000.
- Robert Neff, "Japan's Hidden Hot Springs". Charles E. Tuttle Co., 1995.
- Peter Grill & Dana Levy, "Pleasures of the Japanese Bath". Weatherhill, 1992.
- Sally Clark, "House Beautiful - Bathrooms". Hearst Books, 1999.
- Terence Conran, "Easy Living". Conran Octopus, 1999.
- Barbara Sallick with Lisa Light, "Waterworks - Inventing Bath Style". Clarkson Potter, 2001.
- Jane Withers, "Hot Water - Bathing and the Contemporay Bathroom". Quadrille Publishing, 1999.
- Leonard Koren, "Undesigning the Bath". Stone Bridge Press, 1996.
- Catherine Haig, "Making the Most of Bathrooms". Conran Octopus, 1996.
- Jane Campsie, "Le Bain - Styles d'Aujourd'hui". Könemann, 2001.
- Chris Casson Madden, "Bathrooms". Clarkson Potter, 1996.
- VT Wonen, Jan Des Bouvrie, "Baden". VNU, 1999.
- Julie V. Iovine, "Home - Chic Simple". Thames and Hudson, 1993.
- Piet Boon, "Piet Boon". Terra/Lannoo, 2001.

LEFT
Bathroom by Nathalie Van Reeth.

NEXT
The exclusive pebbles in
this bathroom created by
Yvette Seder come from
Lapidis.

PHOTOGRAPHY
CREDITS

All the photos: Jo Pauwels, except

p. 188-191: Dirk De Keyzer